CHRISTMAS

Party Planner

CHRISTMAS *Party Planner*

LOCATION

TIME

NUMBER OF GUESTS

BUDGET

DATE

THEME

DRESS CODE

KIDS INVITE   YES   NO

SCHEDULE

ACTIVITES / GAMES

TO-DOS

NOTE

CHRISTMAS *Party Planner*

LOCATION

DATE

TIME

THEME

NUMBER OF GUESTS

DRESS CODE

BUDGET

KIDS INVITE YES NO

SCHEDULE

ACTIVITES / GAMES

TO-DOS

NOTE

CHRISTMAS *Party Planner*

LOCATION

DATE

TIME

THEME

NUMBER OF GUESTS

DRESS CODE

BUDGET

KIDS INVITE   YES   NO

SCHEDULE

ACTIVITES / GAMES

TO-DOS

NOTE

CHRISTMAS *Party Planner*

LOCATION

DATE

TIME

THEME

NUMBER OF GUESTS

DRESS CODE

BUDGET

KIDS INVITE　　　○ YES　　　○ NO

SCHEDULE

ACTIVITES / GAMES

TO-DOS

NOTE

CHRISTMAS *Party Planner*

LOCATION	**DATE**
TIME	**THEME**
NUMBER OF GUESTS	**DRESS CODE**
BUDGET	**KIDS INVITE** YES NO

SCHEDULE

ACTIVITES / GAMES

TO-DOS

NOTE

CHRISTMAS *Party Planner*

LOCATION

TIME

NUMBER OF GUESTS

BUDGET

DATE

THEME

DRESS CODE

KIDS INVITE   YES   NO

SCHEDULE

ACTIVITES / GAMES

TO-DOS

NOTE

CHRISTMAS *Party Planner*

LOCATION

TIME

NUMBER OF GUESTS

BUDGET

DATE

THEME

DRESS CODE

KIDS INVITE   YES   NO

SCHEDULE

ACTIVITES / GAMES

TO-DOS

NOTE

CHRISTMAS *Party Planner*

LOCATION

TIME

NUMBER OF GUESTS

BUDGET

DATE

THEME

DRESS CODE

KIDS INVITE   YES   NO

SCHEDULE

ACTIVITES / GAMES

TO-DOS

NOTE

CHRISTMAS *Party Planner*

LOCATION

DATE

TIME

THEME

NUMBER OF GUESTS

DRESS CODE

BUDGET

KIDS INVITE YES NO

SCHEDULE

ACTIVITES / GAMES

TO-DOS

NOTE

CHRISTMAS *Party Planner*

LOCATION

DATE

TIME

THEME

NUMBER OF GUESTS

DRESS CODE

BUDGET

KIDS INVITE   ◌ YES   ◌ NO

SCHEDULE

ACTIVITES / GAMES

TO-DOS

NOTE

CHRISTMAS *Party Planner*

LOCATION

TIME

NUMBER OF GUESTS

BUDGET

DATE

THEME

DRESS CODE

KIDS INVITE YES NO

SCHEDULE

ACTIVITES / GAMES

TO-DOS

NOTE

CHRISTMAS *Party Planner*

LOCATION

TIME

NUMBER OF GUESTS

BUDGET

DATE

THEME

DRESS CODE

KIDS INVITE   ○ YES   ○ NO

SCHEDULE

ACTIVITES / GAMES

TO-DOS

NOTE

CHRISTMAS *Party Planner*

LOCATION

DATE

TIME

THEME

NUMBER OF GUESTS

DRESS CODE

BUDGET

KIDS INVITE YES NO

SCHEDULE

ACTIVITES / GAMES

TO-DOS

NOTE

CHRISTMAS Party Planner

LOCATION

DATE

TIME

THEME

NUMBER OF GUESTS

DRESS CODE

BUDGET

KIDS INVITE   YES   NO

SCHEDULE

ACTIVITES / GAMES

TO-DOS

NOTE

CHRISTMAS *Party Planner*

LOCATION

DATE

TIME

THEME

NUMBER OF GUESTS

DRESS CODE

BUDGET

KIDS INVITE ○ YES ○ NO

SCHEDULE

ACTIVITES / GAMES

TO-DOS

NOTE

CHRISTMAS *Party Planner*

LOCATION

TIME

NUMBER OF GUESTS

BUDGET

DATE

THEME

DRESS CODE

KIDS INVITE   YES   NO

SCHEDULE

ACTIVITES / GAMES

TO-DOS

NOTE

CHRISTMAS *Party Planner*

LOCATION

TIME

NUMBER OF GUESTS

BUDGET

DATE

THEME

DRESS CODE

KIDS INVITE   YES   NO

SCHEDULE

ACTIVITES / GAMES

TO-DOS

NOTE

CHRISTMAS *Party Planner*

LOCATION

TIME

NUMBER OF GUESTS

BUDGET

DATE

THEME

DRESS CODE

KIDS INVITE   ○ YES   ○ NO

SCHEDULE

ACTIVITES / GAMES

- ○
- ○
- ○
- ○
- ○
- ○
- ○
- ○
- ○
- ○

TO-DOS

- ○
- ○
- ○
- ○
- ○
- ○
- ○
- ○
- ○
- ○

NOTE

CHRISTMAS *Party Planner*

LOCATION

TIME

NUMBER OF GUESTS

BUDGET

DATE

THEME

DRESS CODE

KIDS INVITE   YES   NO

SCHEDULE

ACTIVITES / GAMES

TO-DOS

NOTE

CHRISTMAS *Party Planner*

LOCATION

DATE

TIME

THEME

NUMBER OF GUESTS

DRESS CODE

BUDGET

KIDS INVITE   YES   NO

SCHEDULE

ACTIVITES / GAMES

TO-DOS

NOTE

CHRISTMAS *Party Planner*

LOCATION

DATE

TIME

THEME

NUMBER OF GUESTS

DRESS CODE

BUDGET

KIDS INVITE   ○ YES   ○ NO

SCHEDULE

ACTIVITES / GAMES

TO-DOS

NOTE

CHRISTMAS *Party Planner*

LOCATION

TIME

NUMBER OF GUESTS

BUDGET

DATE

THEME

DRESS CODE

KIDS INVITE   YES   NO

SCHEDULE

ACTIVITES / GAMES

TO-DOS

NOTE

CHRISTMAS *Party Planner*

LOCATION

TIME

NUMBER OF GUESTS

BUDGET

DATE

THEME

DRESS CODE

KIDS INVITE YES NO

SCHEDULE

ACTIVITES / GAMES

TO-DOS

NOTE

CHRISTMAS *Party Planner*

LOCATION

TIME

NUMBER OF GUESTS

BUDGET

DATE

THEME

DRESS CODE

KIDS INVITE   YES   NO

SCHEDULE

ACTIVITES / GAMES

TO-DOS

NOTE

CHRISTMAS *Party Planner*

LOCATION

DATE

TIME

THEME

NUMBER OF GUESTS

DRESS CODE

BUDGET

KIDS INVITE   ○ YES   ○ NO

SCHEDULE

ACTIVITES / GAMES

TO-DOS

NOTE

CHRISTMAS *Party Planner*

LOCATION

DATE

TIME

THEME

NUMBER OF GUESTS

DRESS CODE

BUDGET

KIDS INVITE 　　YES　　NO

SCHEDULE

ACTIVITES / GAMES

TO-DOS

NOTE

CHRISTMAS *Party Planner*

LOCATION

DATE

TIME

THEME

NUMBER OF GUESTS

DRESS CODE

BUDGET

KIDS INVITE YES NO

SCHEDULE

ACTIVITES / GAMES

TO-DOS

NOTE

CHRISTMAS *Party Planner*

LOCATION

DATE

TIME

THEME

NUMBER OF GUESTS

DRESS CODE

BUDGET

KIDS INVITE   YES   NO

SCHEDULE

ACTIVITES / GAMES

TO-DOS

NOTE

CHRISTMAS *Party Planner*

LOCATION

TIME

NUMBER OF GUESTS

BUDGET

DATE

THEME

DRESS CODE

KIDS INVITE   YES   NO

SCHEDULE

ACTIVITES / GAMES

TO-DOS

NOTE

CHRISTMAS *Party Planner*

LOCATION

TIME

NUMBER OF GUESTS

BUDGET

DATE

THEME

DRESS CODE

KIDS INVITE　　YES　　NO

SCHEDULE

ACTIVITES / GAMES

TO-DOS

NOTE

CHRISTMAS *Party Planner*

LOCATION

DATE

TIME

THEME

NUMBER OF GUESTS

DRESS CODE

BUDGET

KIDS INVITE   ◯ YES   ◯ NO

SCHEDULE

ACTIVITES / GAMES

TO-DOS

NOTE

CHRISTMAS *Party Planner*

LOCATION

TIME

NUMBER OF GUESTS

BUDGET

DATE

THEME

DRESS CODE

KIDS INVITE   ○ YES   ○ NO

SCHEDULE

ACTIVITES / GAMES

TO-DOS

NOTE

CHRISTMAS *Party Planner*

LOCATION

DATE

TIME

THEME

NUMBER OF GUESTS

DRESS CODE

BUDGET

KIDS INVITE   YES   NO

SCHEDULE

ACTIVITES / GAMES

TO-DOS

NOTE

CHRISTMAS *Party Planner*

LOCATION

DATE

TIME

THEME

NUMBER OF GUESTS

DRESS CODE

BUDGET

KIDS INVITE   YES   NO

SCHEDULE

ACTIVITES / GAMES

TO-DOS

NOTE

CHRISTMAS *Party Planner*

LOCATION

TIME

NUMBER OF GUESTS

BUDGET

DATE

THEME

DRESS CODE

KIDS INVITE   ○ YES   ○ NO

SCHEDULE

ACTIVITES / GAMES

TO-DOS

NOTE

CHRISTMAS *Party Planner*

LOCATION

TIME

NUMBER OF GUESTS

BUDGET

DATE

THEME

DRESS CODE

KIDS INVITE   YES   NO

SCHEDULE

ACTIVITES / GAMES

TO-DOS

NOTE

CHRISTMAS *Party Planner*

LOCATION

TIME

NUMBER OF GUESTS

BUDGET

DATE

THEME

DRESS CODE

KIDS INVITE   YES   NO

SCHEDULE

ACTIVITES / GAMES

TO-DOS

NOTE

CHRISTMAS *Party Planner*

LOCATION

DATE

TIME

THEME

NUMBER OF GUESTS

DRESS CODE

BUDGET

KIDS INVITE   YES   NO

SCHEDULE

ACTIVITES / GAMES

TO-DOS

NOTE

CHRISTMAS *Party Planner*

LOCATION

DATE

TIME

THEME

NUMBER OF GUESTS

DRESS CODE

BUDGET

KIDS INVITE   YES   NO

SCHEDULE

ACTIVITES / GAMES

TO-DOS

NOTE

CHRISTMAS *Party Planner*

LOCATION

TIME

NUMBER OF GUESTS

BUDGET

DATE

THEME

DRESS CODE

KIDS INVITE   YES   NO

SCHEDULE

ACTIVITES / GAMES

TO-DOS

NOTE

CHRISTMAS *Party Planner*

LOCATION	**DATE**
TIME	**THEME**
NUMBER OF GUESTS	**DRESS CODE**
BUDGET	**KIDS INVITE** YES NO

SCHEDULE

ACTIVITES / GAMES

TO-DOS

NOTE

CHRISTMAS *Party Planner*

LOCATION

DATE

TIME

THEME

NUMBER OF GUESTS

DRESS CODE

BUDGET

KIDS INVITE   ○ YES   ○ NO

SCHEDULE

ACTIVITES / GAMES

- ○
- ○
- ○
- ○
- ○
- ○
- ○
- ○
- ○
- ○

TO-DOS

NOTE

CHRISTMAS *Party Planner*

LOCATION

TIME

NUMBER OF GUESTS

BUDGET

DATE

THEME

DRESS CODE

KIDS INVITE   YES   NO

SCHEDULE

ACTIVITES / GAMES

TO-DOS

NOTE

CHRISTMAS *Party Planner*

LOCATION

TIME

NUMBER OF GUESTS

BUDGET

DATE

THEME

DRESS CODE

KIDS INVITE YES NO

SCHEDULE

ACTIVITES / GAMES

TO-DOS

NOTE

CHRISTMAS *Party Planner*

LOCATION

DATE

TIME

THEME

NUMBER OF GUESTS

DRESS CODE

BUDGET

KIDS INVITE   ⬤ YES   ⬤ NO

SCHEDULE

ACTIVITES / GAMES

TO-DOS

NOTE

CHRISTMAS *Party Planner*

LOCATION

DATE

TIME

THEME

NUMBER OF GUESTS

DRESS CODE

BUDGET

KIDS INVITE   ⦿ YES   ⦿ NO

SCHEDULE

ACTIVITES / GAMES

TO-DOS

NOTE

CHRISTMAS *Party Planner*

LOCATION

DATE

TIME

THEME

NUMBER OF GUESTS

DRESS CODE

BUDGET

KIDS INVITE   YES   NO

SCHEDULE

ACTIVITES / GAMES

TO-DOS

NOTE

CHRISTMAS *Party Planner*

LOCATION

DATE

TIME

THEME

NUMBER OF GUESTS

DRESS CODE

BUDGET

KIDS INVITE   YES   NO

SCHEDULE

ACTIVITES / GAMES

TO-DOS

NOTE

CHRISTMAS *Party Planner*

LOCATION

DATE

TIME

THEME

NUMBER OF GUESTS

DRESS CODE

BUDGET

KIDS INVITE   YES   NO

SCHEDULE

ACTIVITES / GAMES

TO-DOS

NOTE

CHRISTMAS *Party Planner*

LOCATION

TIME

NUMBER OF GUESTS

BUDGET

DATE

THEME

DRESS CODE

KIDS INVITE   YES   NO

SCHEDULE

ACTIVITES / GAMES

TO-DOS

NOTE

CHRISTMAS *Party Planner*

LOCATION

DATE

TIME

THEME

NUMBER OF GUESTS

DRESS CODE

BUDGET

KIDS INVITE   YES   NO

SCHEDULE

ACTIVITES / GAMES

TO-DOS

NOTE

CHRISTMAS *Party Planner*

LOCATION

DATE

TIME

THEME

NUMBER OF GUESTS

DRESS CODE

BUDGET

KIDS INVITE   YES   NO

SCHEDULE

ACTIVITES / GAMES

TO-DOS

NOTE

CHRISTMAS *Party Planner*

LOCATION

TIME

NUMBER OF GUESTS

BUDGET

DATE

THEME

DRESS CODE

KIDS INVITE YES NO

SCHEDULE

ACTIVITES / GAMES

TO-DOS

NOTE

CHRISTMAS *Party Planner*

LOCATION

TIME

NUMBER OF GUESTS

BUDGET

DATE

THEME

DRESS CODE

KIDS INVITE   YES   NO

SCHEDULE

ACTIVITES / GAMES

TO-DOS

NOTE

CHRISTMAS *Party Planner*

LOCATION

TIME

NUMBER OF GUESTS

BUDGET

DATE

THEME

DRESS CODE

KIDS INVITE   YES   NO

SCHEDULE

ACTIVITES / GAMES

TO-DOS

NOTE

CHRISTMAS *Party Planner*

LOCATION

DATE

TIME

THEME

NUMBER OF GUESTS

DRESS CODE

BUDGET

KIDS INVITE   ○ YES   ○ NO

SCHEDULE

ACTIVITES / GAMES

TO-DOS

NOTE

CHRISTMAS *Party Planner*

LOCATION

DATE

TIME

THEME

NUMBER OF GUESTS

DRESS CODE

BUDGET

KIDS INVITE   YES   NO

SCHEDULE

ACTIVITES / GAMES

TO-DOS

NOTE

CHRISTMAS *Party Planner*

LOCATION

TIME

NUMBER OF GUESTS

BUDGET

DATE

THEME

DRESS CODE

KIDS INVITE   ○ YES   ○ NO

SCHEDULE

ACTIVITES / GAMES

TO-DOS

NOTE

CHRISTMAS *Party Planner*

LOCATION

DATE

TIME

THEME

NUMBER OF GUESTS

DRESS CODE

BUDGET

KIDS INVITE   YES   NO

SCHEDULE

ACTIVITES / GAMES

TO-DOS

NOTE

CHRISTMAS *Party Planner*

LOCATION

DATE

TIME

THEME

NUMBER OF GUESTS

DRESS CODE

BUDGET

KIDS INVITE   YES   NO

SCHEDULE

ACTIVITES / GAMES

TO-DOS

NOTE

CHRISTMAS *Party Planner*

LOCATION

DATE

TIME

THEME

NUMBER OF GUESTS

DRESS CODE

BUDGET

KIDS INVITE   YES   NO

SCHEDULE

ACTIVITES / GAMES

TO-DOS

NOTE

CHRISTMAS *Party Planner*

LOCATION

DATE

TIME

THEME

NUMBER OF GUESTS

DRESS CODE

BUDGET

KIDS INVITE   YES   NO

SCHEDULE

ACTIVITES / GAMES

TO-DOS

NOTE

CHRISTMAS *Party Planner*

LOCATION

DATE

TIME

THEME

NUMBER OF GUESTS

DRESS CODE

BUDGET

KIDS INVITE   YES   NO

SCHEDULE

ACTIVITES / GAMES

TO-DOS

NOTE

CHRISTMAS *Party Planner*

LOCATION

TIME

NUMBER OF GUESTS

BUDGET

DATE

THEME

DRESS CODE

KIDS INVITE   YES   NO

SCHEDULE

ACTIVITES / GAMES

TO-DOS

NOTE

CHRISTMAS Party Planner

LOCATION

TIME

NUMBER OF GUESTS

BUDGET

DATE

THEME

DRESS CODE

KIDS INVITE   YES   NO

SCHEDULE

ACTIVITES / GAMES

TO-DOS

NOTE

CHRISTMAS *Party Planner*

LOCATION

DATE

TIME

THEME

NUMBER OF GUESTS

DRESS CODE

BUDGET

KIDS INVITE   YES   NO

SCHEDULE

ACTIVITES / GAMES

TO-DOS

NOTE

CHRISTMAS *Party Planner*

LOCATION

DATE

TIME

THEME

NUMBER OF GUESTS

DRESS CODE

BUDGET

KIDS INVITE   YES   NO

SCHEDULE

ACTIVITES / GAMES

TO-DOS

NOTE

CHRISTMAS *Party Planner*

LOCATION

TIME

NUMBER OF GUESTS

BUDGET

DATE

THEME

DRESS CODE

KIDS INVITE ○ YES ○ NO

SCHEDULE

ACTIVITES / GAMES

TO-DOS

NOTE

CHRISTMAS *Party Planner*

LOCATION

TIME

NUMBER OF GUESTS

BUDGET

DATE

THEME

DRESS CODE

KIDS INVITE   YES   NO

SCHEDULE

ACTIVITES / GAMES

TO-DOS

NOTE

CHRISTMAS *Party Planner*

LOCATION

TIME

NUMBER OF GUESTS

BUDGET

DATE

THEME

DRESS CODE

KIDS INVITE   YES   NO

SCHEDULE

ACTIVITES / GAMES

TO-DOS

NOTE

CHRISTMAS *Party Planner*

LOCATION

DATE

TIME

THEME

NUMBER OF GUESTS

DRESS CODE

BUDGET

KIDS INVITE   YES   NO

SCHEDULE

ACTIVITES / GAMES

TO-DOS

NOTE

CHRISTMAS *Party Planner*

LOCATION

TIME

NUMBER OF GUESTS

BUDGET

DATE

THEME

DRESS CODE

KIDS INVITE   ⚪ YES   ⚪ NO

SCHEDULE

ACTIVITES / GAMES

TO-DOS

NOTE

CHRISTMAS *Party Planner*

LOCATION

TIME

NUMBER OF GUESTS

BUDGET

DATE

THEME

DRESS CODE

KIDS INVITE   YES   NO

SCHEDULE

ACTIVITES / GAMES

TO-DOS

NOTE

CHRISTMAS *Party Planner*

LOCATION

TIME

NUMBER OF GUESTS

BUDGET

DATE

THEME

DRESS CODE

KIDS INVITE   YES   NO

SCHEDULE

ACTIVITES / GAMES

TO-DOS

NOTE

CHRISTMAS *Party Planner*

LOCATION

TIME

NUMBER OF GUESTS

BUDGET

DATE

THEME

DRESS CODE

KIDS INVITE   YES   NO

SCHEDULE

ACTIVITES / GAMES

TO-DOS

NOTE

CHRISTMAS *Party Planner*

LOCATION

DATE

TIME

THEME

NUMBER OF GUESTS

DRESS CODE

BUDGET

KIDS INVITE   YES   NO

SCHEDULE

ACTIVITES / GAMES

TO-DOS

NOTE

CHRISTMAS *Party Planner*

LOCATION	DATE
TIME	THEME
NUMBER OF GUESTS	DRESS CODE
BUDGET	KIDS INVITE YES NO

SCHEDULE

ACTIVITES / GAMES

TO-DOS

NOTE

CHRISTMAS *Party Planner*

LOCATION

DATE

TIME

THEME

NUMBER OF GUESTS

DRESS CODE

BUDGET

KIDS INVITE   YES   NO

SCHEDULE

ACTIVITES / GAMES

TO-DOS

NOTE

CHRISTMAS *Party Planner*

LOCATION

DATE

TIME

THEME

NUMBER OF GUESTS

DRESS CODE

BUDGET

KIDS INVITE   YES   NO

SCHEDULE

ACTIVITES / GAMES

TO-DOS

NOTE

CHRISTMAS *Party Planner*

LOCATION

DATE

TIME

THEME

NUMBER OF GUESTS

DRESS CODE

BUDGET

KIDS INVITE YES NO

SCHEDULE

ACTIVITES / GAMES

TO-DOS

NOTE

CHRISTMAS *Party Planner*

LOCATION

TIME

NUMBER OF GUESTS

BUDGET

DATE

THEME

DRESS CODE

KIDS INVITE YES NO

SCHEDULE

ACTIVITES / GAMES

TO-DOS

NOTE

CHRISTMAS *Party Planner*

LOCATION

TIME

NUMBER OF GUESTS

BUDGET

DATE

THEME

DRESS CODE

KIDS INVITE   YES   NO

SCHEDULE

ACTIVITES / GAMES

TO-DOS

NOTE

CHRISTMAS *Party Planner*

LOCATION

TIME

NUMBER OF GUESTS

BUDGET

DATE

THEME

DRESS CODE

KIDS INVITE YES NO

SCHEDULE

ACTIVITES / GAMES

TO-DOS

NOTE

CHRISTMAS *Party Planner*

LOCATION

TIME

NUMBER OF GUESTS

BUDGET

DATE

THEME

DRESS CODE

KIDS INVITE   YES   NO

SCHEDULE

ACTIVITES / GAMES

TO-DOS

NOTE

CHRISTMAS *Party Planner*

LOCATION

TIME

NUMBER OF GUESTS

BUDGET

DATE

THEME

DRESS CODE

KIDS INVITE   YES   NO

SCHEDULE

ACTIVITES / GAMES

TO-DOS

NOTE

CHRISTMAS *Party Planner*

LOCATION

DATE

TIME

THEME

NUMBER OF GUESTS

DRESS CODE

BUDGET

KIDS INVITE   ○ YES   ○ NO

SCHEDULE

ACTIVITES / GAMES

TO-DOS

NOTE

CHRISTMAS *Party Planner*

LOCATION

DATE

TIME

THEME

NUMBER OF GUESTS

DRESS CODE

BUDGET

KIDS INVITE   YES   NO

SCHEDULE

ACTIVITES / GAMES

TO-DOS

NOTE

CHRISTMAS *Party Planner*

LOCATION

DATE

TIME

THEME

NUMBER OF GUESTS

DRESS CODE

BUDGET

KIDS INVITE   YES   NO

SCHEDULE

ACTIVITES / GAMES

TO-DOS

NOTE

CHRISTMAS *Party Planner*

LOCATION

DATE

TIME

THEME

NUMBER OF GUESTS

DRESS CODE

BUDGET

KIDS INVITE YES NO

SCHEDULE

ACTIVITES / GAMES

TO-DOS

NOTE

CHRISTMAS *Party Planner*

LOCATION

TIME

NUMBER OF GUESTS

BUDGET

DATE

THEME

DRESS CODE

KIDS INVITE   YES   NO

SCHEDULE

ACTIVITES / GAMES

TO-DOS

NOTE

CHRISTMAS *Party Planner*

LOCATION	**DATE**
TIME	**THEME**
NUMBER OF GUESTS	**DRESS CODE**
BUDGET	**KIDS INVITE** YES NO

SCHEDULE

ACTIVITES / GAMES

TO-DOS

NOTE

CHRISTMAS *Party Planner*

LOCATION

DATE

TIME

THEME

NUMBER OF GUESTS

DRESS CODE

BUDGET

KIDS INVITE   ○ YES   ○ NO

SCHEDULE

ACTIVITES / GAMES

TO-DOS

NOTE

CHRISTMAS *Party Planner*

LOCATION

TIME

NUMBER OF GUESTS

BUDGET

DATE

THEME

DRESS CODE

KIDS INVITE   ○ YES   ○ NO

SCHEDULE

ACTIVITES / GAMES

TO-DOS

NOTE

CHRISTMAS *Party Planner*

LOCATION

DATE

TIME

THEME

NUMBER OF GUESTS

DRESS CODE

BUDGET

KIDS INVITE   YES   NO

SCHEDULE

ACTIVITES / GAMES

TO-DOS

NOTE

CHRISTMAS *Party Planner*

LOCATION

TIME

NUMBER OF GUESTS

BUDGET

DATE

THEME

DRESS CODE

KIDS INVITE   YES   NO

SCHEDULE

ACTIVITES / GAMES

TO-DOS

NOTE

CHRISTMAS *Party Planner*

LOCATION

TIME

NUMBER OF GUESTS

BUDGET

DATE

THEME

DRESS CODE

KIDS INVITE   YES   NO

SCHEDULE

ACTIVITES / GAMES

TO-DOS

NOTE

CHRISTMAS *Party Planner*

LOCATION

DATE

TIME

THEME

NUMBER OF GUESTS

DRESS CODE

BUDGET

KIDS INVITE   YES   NO

SCHEDULE

ACTIVITES / GAMES

TO-DOS

NOTE

CHRISTMAS *Party Planner*

LOCATION

DATE

TIME

THEME

NUMBER OF GUESTS

DRESS CODE

BUDGET

KIDS INVITE   YES   NO

SCHEDULE

ACTIVITES / GAMES

TO-DOS

NOTE

CHRISTMAS *Party Planner*

LOCATION

TIME

NUMBER OF GUESTS

BUDGET

DATE

THEME

DRESS CODE

KIDS INVITE   YES   NO

SCHEDULE

ACTIVITES / GAMES

TO-DOS

NOTE

CHRISTMAS *Party Planner*

LOCATION

DATE

TIME

THEME

NUMBER OF GUESTS

DRESS CODE

BUDGET

KIDS INVITE   ○ YES   ○ NO

SCHEDULE

ACTIVITES / GAMES

TO-DOS

NOTE

CHRISTMAS *Party Planner*

LOCATION

DATE

TIME

THEME

NUMBER OF GUESTS

DRESS CODE

BUDGET

KIDS INVITE   ○ YES   ○ NO

SCHEDULE

ACTIVITES / GAMES

TO-DOS

NOTE

CHRISTMAS *Party Planner*

LOCATION

DATE

TIME

THEME

NUMBER OF GUESTS

DRESS CODE

BUDGET

KIDS INVITE   YES   NO

SCHEDULE

ACTIVITES / GAMES

TO-DOS

NOTE

CHRISTMAS *Party Planner*

LOCATION	**DATE**
TIME	**THEME**
NUMBER OF GUESTS	**DRESS CODE**
BUDGET	**KIDS INVITE** YES NO

SCHEDULE

ACTIVITES / GAMES

TO-DOS

NOTE

CHRISTMAS *Party Planner*

LOCATION

TIME

NUMBER OF GUESTS

BUDGET

DATE

THEME

DRESS CODE

KIDS INVITE   ○ YES   ○ NO

SCHEDULE

ACTIVITES / GAMES

TO-DOS

NOTE

CHRISTMAS *Party Planner*

LOCATION

TIME

NUMBER OF GUESTS

BUDGET

DATE

THEME

DRESS CODE

KIDS INVITE   YES   NO

SCHEDULE

ACTIVITES / GAMES

TO-DOS

NOTE

CHRISTMAS Party Planner

LOCATION

TIME

NUMBER OF GUESTS

BUDGET

DATE

THEME

DRESS CODE

KIDS INVITE YES NO

SCHEDULE

ACTIVITES / GAMES

TO-DOS

NOTE

CHRISTMAS *Party Planner*

LOCATION

DATE

TIME

THEME

NUMBER OF GUESTS

DRESS CODE

BUDGET

KIDS INVITE   YES   NO

SCHEDULE

ACTIVITES / GAMES

TO-DOS

NOTE

CHRISTMAS *Party Planner*

LOCATION

DATE

TIME

THEME

NUMBER OF GUESTS

DRESS CODE

BUDGET

KIDS INVITE   YES   NO

SCHEDULE

ACTIVITES / GAMES

TO-DOS

NOTE

CHRISTMAS *Party Planner*

LOCATION

TIME

NUMBER OF GUESTS

BUDGET

DATE

THEME

DRESS CODE

KIDS INVITE   YES   NO

SCHEDULE

ACTIVITES / GAMES

TO-DOS

NOTE

CHRISTMAS *Party Planner*

LOCATION

DATE

TIME

THEME

NUMBER OF GUESTS

DRESS CODE

BUDGET

KIDS INVITE   YES   NO

SCHEDULE

ACTIVITES / GAMES

TO-DOS

NOTE

CHRISTMAS *Party Planner*

LOCATION

TIME

NUMBER OF GUESTS

BUDGET

DATE

THEME

DRESS CODE

KIDS INVITE YES NO

SCHEDULE

ACTIVITES / GAMES

TO-DOS

NOTE

CHRISTMAS *Party Planner*

LOCATION

DATE

TIME

THEME

NUMBER OF GUESTS

DRESS CODE

BUDGET

KIDS INVITE   YES   NO

SCHEDULE

ACTIVITES / GAMES

TO-DOS

NOTE

CHRISTMAS *Party Planner*

LOCATION

TIME

NUMBER OF GUESTS

BUDGET

DATE

THEME

DRESS CODE

KIDS INVITE   YES   NO

SCHEDULE

ACTIVITES / GAMES

TO-DOS

NOTE

CHRISTMAS *Party Planner*

LOCATION

DATE

TIME

THEME

NUMBER OF GUESTS

DRESS CODE

BUDGET

KIDS INVITE   YES   NO

SCHEDULE

ACTIVITES / GAMES

TO-DOS

NOTE

CHRISTMAS *Party Planner*

LOCATION

DATE

TIME

THEME

NUMBER OF GUESTS

DRESS CODE

BUDGET

KIDS INVITE   YES   NO

SCHEDULE

ACTIVITES / GAMES

TO-DOS

NOTE

CHRISTMAS *Party Planner*

LOCATION

DATE

TIME

THEME

NUMBER OF GUESTS

DRESS CODE

BUDGET

KIDS INVITE   YES   NO

SCHEDULE

ACTIVITES / GAMES

TO-DOS

NOTE

CHRISTMAS *Party Planner*

LOCATION

DATE

TIME

THEME

NUMBER OF GUESTS

DRESS CODE

BUDGET

KIDS INVITE   YES   NO

SCHEDULE

ACTIVITES / GAMES

TO-DOS

NOTE

CHRISTMAS *Party Planner*

LOCATION

TIME

NUMBER OF GUESTS

BUDGET

DATE

THEME

DRESS CODE

KIDS INVITE   YES   NO

SCHEDULE

ACTIVITES / GAMES

TO-DOS

NOTE

CHRISTMAS *Party Planner*

LOCATION

DATE

TIME

THEME

NUMBER OF GUESTS

DRESS CODE

BUDGET

KIDS INVITE   YES   NO

SCHEDULE

ACTIVITES / GAMES

TO-DOS

NOTE

CHRISTMAS *Party Planner*

LOCATION

DATE

TIME

THEME

NUMBER OF GUESTS

DRESS CODE

BUDGET

KIDS INVITE   YES   NO

SCHEDULE

ACTIVITES / GAMES

TO-DOS

NOTE

CHRISTMAS *Party Planner*

LOCATION

TIME

NUMBER OF GUESTS

BUDGET

DATE

THEME

DRESS CODE

KIDS INVITE   ◌ YES   ◌ NO

SCHEDULE

ACTIVITES / GAMES

TO-DOS

NOTE

CHRISTMAS *Party Planner*

LOCATION

DATE

TIME

THEME

NUMBER OF GUESTS

DRESS CODE

BUDGET

KIDS INVITE   ◯ YES   ◯ NO

SCHEDULE

ACTIVITES / GAMES

TO-DOS

NOTE

CHRISTMAS *Party Planner*

LOCATION

DATE

TIME

THEME

NUMBER OF GUESTS

DRESS CODE

BUDGET

KIDS INVITE   YES   NO

SCHEDULE

ACTIVITES / GAMES

TO-DOS

NOTE

CHRISTMAS *Party Planner*

LOCATION

TIME

NUMBER OF GUESTS

BUDGET

DATE

THEME

DRESS CODE

KIDS INVITE YES NO

SCHEDULE

ACTIVITES / GAMES

TO-DOS

NOTE

CHRISTMAS *Party Planner*

LOCATION

TIME

NUMBER OF GUESTS

BUDGET

DATE

THEME

DRESS CODE

KIDS INVITE   YES   NO

SCHEDULE

ACTIVITES / GAMES

TO-DOS

NOTE

CHRISTMAS *Party Planner*

LOCATION

DATE

TIME

THEME

NUMBER OF GUESTS

DRESS CODE

BUDGET

KIDS INVITE   YES   NO

SCHEDULE

ACTIVITES / GAMES

TO-DOS

NOTE

CHRISTMAS *Party Planner*

LOCATION

DATE

TIME

THEME

NUMBER OF GUESTS

DRESS CODE

BUDGET

KIDS INVITE   ○ YES   ○ NO

SCHEDULE

ACTIVITES / GAMES

TO-DOS

NOTE

CHRISTMAS *Party Planner*

LOCATION

TIME

NUMBER OF GUESTS

BUDGET

DATE

THEME

DRESS CODE

KIDS INVITE   YES   NO

SCHEDULE

ACTIVITES / GAMES

TO-DOS

NOTE

CHRISTMAS *Party Planner*

LOCATION

TIME

NUMBER OF GUESTS

BUDGET

DATE

THEME

DRESS CODE

KIDS INVITE   YES   NO

SCHEDULE

ACTIVITES / GAMES

TO-DOS

NOTE

CHRISTMAS *Party Planner*

LOCATION

TIME

NUMBER OF GUESTS

BUDGET

DATE

THEME

DRESS CODE

KIDS INVITE   YES   NO

SCHEDULE

ACTIVITES / GAMES

TO-DOS

NOTE

www.ingramcontent.com/pod-product-compliance
Lightning Source LLC
Chambersburg PA
CBHW040144110726
48005CB00018B/2641